Second Wave

Poems

by

Joseph V. Ricapito

BORDIGHERA PRESS

Library of Congress Control Number: 2008930700

Cover artwork: *St. Martin Hotel Street* and *Barca di pesca*,
by Anthony V. Cervone

© 2008 by Joseph V. Ricapito

All rights reserved. Parts of this book may be reprinted only by written permission from the authors, and may not be reproduced for publication in book, magazine, or electronic media of any kind, except in quotations for purposes of literary reviews by critics.

Printed in the United States.

Published by
BORDIGHERA PRESS
John D. Calandra Italian American Institute
25 West 43rd Street, 17th Floor
New York, NY 10036

VIA FOLIOS 52
ISBN 1-884419-98-4

*to Martha and Michael De Marco,
with much love.*

Second Wave

POEMS

Double Scorpio	7
Obon Festival	8
Academia	9
Aftermath	10
He asked "Why do you want your ashes buried at sea?"	11
Bernard Malamud (1914–1986)	12
Birthday Girl	13
Changes	14
Yet to Come	15
The Island of Crete I	16
The Island of Crete II	17
The Island of Crete III	18
The Island of Crete IV	19
The Island of Crete V	20
Divorce House	21
The Dove Dead	22
The Remnant Shop on Eighth Avenue	23
Father and Son	24
Florence City	25
Flying	26
Age	27
Furlough	28
A Giacometti Nude	29
Grief We Lived with and Were Left with	30
A Day Best Not Remembered	32
Harvey Hammond Comes Home	33
Indiana Winter	35
Japanese Tourists in Forence	36
Mid Sixties	37
What Was Missing?	38
My Horn, Now Only Shiny	39
Never to Forget	40
Pittura	41
Poems	42
Polish Mass, Christmas Morning Brooklyn, New York, 1996	43
Revelation	45
The Never-Ending Sea	46

Sex Indulgence	47
Sixty Years Later	48
Southern Lady	49
The Synagogue of Florence, Italy	
Dachau	50
Vietnam 2	51
Never Worn Wedding Dress	
White with Train, Size 8	52
Christmas at Rest Haven Acres	53
Golden Age	55
Behind the Counter at Scherz's Bakery	56
Hearing and Seeing	57
Buddha in Church	58
Indiana Summer Night	59
On Jewry	60
Making Poetry	61
After Fray Luis de León	62
Phantom Garden	65
Old Photograph	66
On the Loss of Virginity	67
A Visit to the Synagogue of Florence	68
Self-Effacement of a Yoga Teacher	69
Five Autobiographical Poems	
I: Initial Visions	70
II: Next Day	71
III: Walking Along	72
IV: At Night	73
V: Family Feasts	74
Cría cuervos para que te saquen los ojos	75
Under the Catalpa Tree	76
Witness	77
Kent State	79
First Communion	80
A Fallen God	83
A Wedding	84
About the Poet	87

Second Wave

DOUBLE SCORPIO

She throws it down, my life, past, present, future, drawn in circles,
initialed and marked with signs, it spins on the table
and comes to rest,
the house of Pluto,
stares at me, stonefaced.

Your signs are good, she says, cautiously,
power, strength, passion, but look out,
—and her face stiffens—
your pettiness and hidden cruelties, manipulating people, you bastard,
and you think you're so good.
Look out! It's Pluto ascending in your fifth house.

That's like a mugger waiting for you in the dark,
and Mars, blood rushing out of his eyes in iron intensity.
You will choke on the wrath that rises up inside
and your smile will shed red light.
In your sixth house a stranger waits.
The darkness of his soul will take you by the hand up,
up through stars.

Ricapito

Obon Festival

These little boats
float on the river
to carry thoughts and wishes,
to renew love,
to remind you that I still
love you.
Guided by colored lanterns
on the whim of the sea,
they head for your abode.
I can't see you,
I touch you with these little cakes
that you loved so much.
I have in my thoughts
the picture of you, your face
lighting up at the taste.
In this boat
my soul is cut in sections
you can have the one
devoted to love.
I give it to no one else.

Second Wave

ACADEMIA

You float along,
Your intent hidden behind the
whir of a psychedelic umbrella.

Your eyes find
grass blades, wounded, now defenseless,
their long spines broken.

Your robust laugh rings out,
behind it
a tense and frightened anticipation.

I shake your hand and feel
the ice in your empty heart
like a thin silver knife
stab my baby, baby soul.

How do you paint the face of treachery?

Ricapito

Aftermath

Who would look at her?
Grey, her legs swollen,
veins traveling around
like complicated wiring.
She can't walk far,
but everyone knows
what an intellect she has.
Her husband teaches science;
he has his head to a microscope most of the time.

At a conference she meets this fellow,
young-ish, a bohemian, he quotes poetry;
smart too.
After dinner and cocktails
he suggests they go to his room
Knees shaking, she feels dread
in the pit of her stomach.
Says yes with sophistication.
They would speak about philosophy.

She didn't want to but she did.
It was a mistake, she knew.
Doesn't everybody do it some time or other,
a thousand miles away?

Going home her thoughts
bounced around
like the plane in the sky.
She dreaded getting off and going home.

How was it? Fine, she said.
And closed herself in her room.

Second Wave

HE ASKED "WHY DO YOU WANT YOUR ASHES BURIED AT SEA?"

Spread my ashes in the sea.
Let them settle
where others have been before.
Let them join ancient civilizations.
Find comfort among sea gods,
travel in marine depths
going from country to country on sea horses.
There, meet old friends,
There, reside until
the time they are given
another life,
another chance.

Ricapito

BERNARD MALAMUD (1914–1986)

He is gone forever,
this chronicler of Jews.
This ghost and haunter
of hidden corners.
No more about birds
who talk,
or Jewish cabbies in Russia,
lamenting their lives
the same as somebody
you would meet on the subway.

His precinct was the world
and those who toiled day to day,
peddlers, salesmen who carried
their wares on their backs like a snail its shell,
solitary people like the old lady
who came each morning at dawn to buy
one single bagel.

No point in leafing through
the pages of book reviews.
There will be no more
novels I rush out to get.
In his picture I see an older man,
a brush moustache on his
upper lip.
He was envied by Jews
and Italians alike.
He understood the codes in their souls;
they did not always like it.
He left Borough Park for Vermont
but his spirit lives
in Brooklyn.

Second Wave

BIRTHDAY GIRL

How neat you look!
Your curls sit
on your shoulders
with planned insouciance,
hands clasped,
lips slightly moist,
eyes smile behind
granny glasses.
Your dress is dated.
Gingham with flowers
and at the hem
some lace
You smile pertly
as people come by
and tap you
lightly on the shoulder,

friends, well-wishers.
You blush,
Everyone has commented
on how grown up you look

and you are thirty-five.

Ricapito

CHANGES

He tried to change himself
the way one day
you decide to put on
a clean shirt and tie
after years of grunge.
But it didn't work.

His father often said
what you were stayed with you.
The fact is that at fifty
you are what you were at five,
or so Freud says.
He went through many transformations
but in the end
he sat silently in a corner remembering
when as a boy
he went out to play
wearing a sailor suit
with a white collar
one day in early fall
and it felt so good.

Second Wave

Yet to Come

I would like to know your children
yet to come
but there may not be time
and so I have created your son
a blond pink-faced child
who runs everywhere
with the nervous movements
of a rabbit
or your daughter with cheeks
like apples
her smile like the sun.
I read them stories and play-act tales
of places I have never been
like China and India.
I see them make their first communion
and graduate from schools and
then they are bright young adults
it is then that they
pay homage to that grandfather
about whose adventures
they heard
but now he is long since gone
long since gone.

Ricapito

THE ISLAND OF CRETE
I

We walk along the pier.
Fishing boats have just returned
from a night's work.
The nets spew forth their catch
of smooth-bellied fish,
some still quivering in the killing air,
others resigned.
The eyes of a giant red snapper bulge out
grotesquely as the fisherman tries to sell it.
It lies there harnessed by a rope,
giant, contorted,
near him another fisherman
throws an octopus against the cement wall
maybe a hundred times.

At the end of the pier two boats sit
in silence and inactivity.
Black flags adorn the ropes of the mast.
On the pier the nets are piled and covered
by a tarp and crowned with a black flag.
No work for a day or two,
and the boats rock slowly
back and forth to the incoming waves.

Second Wave

THE ISLAND OF CRETE
II

Fisherman mend their nets
or shave by pier-side,
harlequins with cream on half their faces.
The tourists carrying knapsacks trudge past
wearied by the sun.

At the end of the quai
a fortress sits squat as a boxer.
Its turrets symmetrical
against the sky.
Their stones are dull and grey.

Now Germans and Brits make a pilgrimage
to where they fought,
each trying to kill the other.
They sit in a café
nursing beers, both sunburned
the skin pink at the
edge of their sleeves.
These two strangers
talk of the drachma
and a place to get good squid.
A jet flies over breaking the sound barrier
as waiters rush to keep the tablecloths in place.
They both grin.

Ricapito

THE ISLAND OF CRETE
III

After Góngora's *Polyphemus*

The mountains are fairly hidden by clouds.
Soon the fog will burn off and the mountains
Will find their reflection in the greenish-blue water.
I watch Polyphemus hovering behind the brush.
I see him as he stalks the mountains and
Grasps easy prey and devours them.
A lamb is but a speck before his large
Reflective eye.
His brothers the satyrs play and frolic.
They leave the imprint of their cloven hooves
In the soft, damp earth.
Having eaten, Polyphemus lies on
The side of the mountain
And dreams of a beautiful goddess
With clean, soft breasts.
In his mind he holds her
Against his hard body.
It is soon time to retreat back to his lair.
As light begins to filter
I lose sight of him and turn to my book
About the beauty of Greece.

Second Wave

THE ISLAND OF CRETE
IV

It has been a long night's work.
She sits dock-side and has a final coffee.
She is but a girl, comes from one of the
Smaller islands.
And now she cruises pier-side.
Life is good on days the big ships come in.

An American ship disgorges young sailors,
Red-headed, freckled, even their tattoos are innocent.
She has learned never to look too long at a face.
She might find love there
And the beginning of a new life.
Better not to hope.
Just undress and hold him between her legs.
She had seven sailors last night.
She feels rich and will buy
The polka dot dress she saw in a shop.
Maybe she will write the name of each sailor
In the dots.
Each dot a dream.

Now she tells her friend
About the sailor who offered
Her a jewel if she would go to America with him.
Together they look at the dark murky coffee
Knowing it is a lie.

Ricapito

THE ISLAND OF CRETE
V

It must be a very hard scrabble
What do the goats and sheep find
between the rocks?
Pebbles rise to rocks and finally
to a towering mountain.
Olive trees on the sides of mountains
are sentinels,
their tortured trunks bespeak
the travail of sucking moisture
out of the parched earth.
Each twist records a century of pain.
Even the leaves never burst into green,
always dull, flat,
the olives are eyes
decorating the sparse branches
until the time they fall,
and bent-over farmers come and fill
sacks.
Later the final indignity
is to be crushed ruthlessly,
but then isn't life this way?

Their brother the fig tree
suffers the same fate.
It finds any pretext to plant its seed
I have seen midget branches sprout
between the stones of the Coliseum,
between the cracks of the sidewalk,
on top of a tower in Lucca.
Like the olive
it plays a deceptive game.
You would never believe it is
a fruit unless you split it open.
With its succulent redness
ultimately it has won.

Second Wave

Divorce House

Can't you tell?
Weeds overrun
the flower beds and a light was left burning,
Shadows move inside.
The gas has been disconnected,
and paint is peeling
along the carpentered eaves.

The porch has developed
a very long face.

Visitors stay away.
The wind chimes
scream when the breeze
blows by.
Next to the driveway
a sign reads
House For Sale.

Ricapito

THE DOVE DEAD

The sky is blue through laziness
As the dove sails air at midday.
Its eyes are ardent
And its beak determined.
Flight is light and lofty,
Its feathers cleaned to pearly white.
It lowers itself
Steadily
Near houses, trees and hedges
Barely touching the world.

It looked back over its wing
A truck snapped into its path
And left it
Stamped on the road
Red and white.

Second Wave

THE REMNANT SHOP ON EIGHTH AVENUE

He insisted
the place had to be dark.
A single light and bolts of cloth, miles of it.
Buttons, clips, belt buckles.

I stood outside lots of times,
watching people walk by
or I would read the newspaper
from cover to cover.

"Be a doctor," mother said.
"Look at Uncle Manny."
I started out trying, as God knows,
but the equations never worked out.
The chemical solutions broke down.
They told me,
"Look for something else."

"Be an officer, be smart."
We ran all day, up all night.
Commands were barked at us,
up and down, up and down.
"Drop down and give me fifty pushups."
At twenty eight I collapsed.
"Sonny, we got a job for you in the supply room."

I tried sales but the cars never moved,
the Xerox machines never sold.
After men's suits and women's clothing shut down
I looked for other things.

"Come on home. I've got the thing for you.
Didn't I raise a family on it?"
Papa gave me the key
which weighed in my hand.
I opened the door
and I heard my life closing ahead of me.

Ricapito

FATHER AND SON

You hold me at the window.
In the evening the only light is from a street lamp.

The falling snow makes the light blue;
The snow falls and falls.
I hold my arm around your head
and watch the snow build atop a car.
I held tightly to your head and my fingers find your ear.
A lonely person trudges up the street,
drags his feet on the wet sidewalk.

I feel the light enter the house,
and we are all suffused with it.

Those few minutes before I sleep
I feel the touch of you still on my fingers
and in old age as I see snow
the touch of you remains on
fingers of silk.

Second Wave

FLORENCE CITY

The sound of motorbikes
Creates a long tunnel of pain.
The cross atop the church
Asks for respite.
God must be patient.
The world has its own agenda,
Oblivious to Michelangelo
And Giotto.
A cab driver tries to explain
To German tourists
That he can't go down the street.
They don't understand.
An American reaches up and
Delicately touches
Ghiberti's masterpiece.
The buses line up like
Sheep mounting one another.

Only at night, alone can I find grace.
In the street,
In a long and silent courtyard
Unmoved, static,
Joyful.

Ricapito

FLYING

Nothing like flying a plane in a storm
to realize you're one step away from ashes.
Every dip and turn sends a gasp to your throat.
Will we arrive?
Folks, you're just ten minutes away from Baton Rouge.
Ten hours.
The stewardess is trained to smile
no matter what.
But her pinched eyes tell me
she's praying.
Another dip and I recite my prayer to St. Joseph.
It's like falling down a chute
until you're buffeted by another twist.
Suddenly it's calm and we angle into the airport lane.
The man next to me has finished the page he was reading.
My breathing restored,
I walk down the aisle.
At the door the pilot
has an actor's moustache on his lip.
I tell him you should be given a prize
for landing this mosquito in that pea soup.
"Aw, shucks," he says, shuffling his feet,
"twarn't nuthin'. Come see us again."
I walk off the plane strong, arrogant like John Wayne.
In my pocket St. Joseph muffles a laugh.

Second Wave

AGE

Forty One 41
looks like a pregnant pole
looking to the west

the students don't share
their smut with me.

Mr. Ricapito
Mr. Ricapito

But they talk of beavers
biting
and then titter

My students smile slyly
when I postured about sex
The old dog!
The old dog!

41

The young woman
with her minuscule
but sensuous tits
hungers for love at 21

a submissive cipher

at 25
she will be satisfied
until at 30 sick and tired

at 41
she will burst

Ricapito

FURLOUGH

It was the first time
he had seen me in uniform.
He waited for me in the art nouveau subway station.
Dressed for work, wearing his every day hat,
he flushed when I stepped through the doors
in an ill-fitting great coat.
In his stare I saw the reflection
of himself forty years before,
puttees, a rumpled field jacket,
wandering around Paris,
hot on the trail of painted-up girls.
Better live it up before going back to the trenches,
putrescence, rats, and fear.
He wondered if he would have to
return to the front
perhaps never to see his mother again.
I never had any of that
only imagined the devastation of war
with harmless, make-believe.

From my room, concealed, I spy him
trying on my fatigues and hats.
He succumbs to a torrent of tears
as he remembers the remains
of one-time buddies.
To his dying day, he remembered Paris,
Verdun and St. Mihiel
and the day he returned home,
his father waiting at the door,
tears of joy on his face.

Second Wave

A Giacometti Nude

The light cuts a swath across your face
Without stretching you reach the sky
Your soul is in your hands
which you hold in a
eucharistic pose
Naked
everything in the room stops
Your legs although immobile
are ready to move
Your limbs are thin
so brittle
your stomach flat
the dark triangle of hair is
alive for it too is ready to spring

The faltering light of afternoon
shades your body
resting until there is no light at all
you will sleep through
rays of light and heavy darkness.

Ricapito

GRIEF WE LIVED WITH AND WERE LEFT WITH

I
I see only shadows
of profiles silent, contours in solemnity

One by one they go,
taking their hope, their life,
everything

Jack, then Bobby
and Medgar and Dr. King
and Schwerner, Goodman and Cheney
and the little girls in a church
(how many are still buried there?)
all file by
History soiled by the offspring of its
own corrupted inventions.

II
Jack's vivacity is written in his Irish face
Round eyes and square-faced
we grieve his loss
And so it goes
The earth is emptied
      (continued)

Second Wave

horribly, ironically, of its power.
The ground becomes hard and stony
we'll not see the sun for a time yet to come

Over the hill the mass of followers,
now bereft of its guides,
flow in waves
their banner raging peace

As the train slowly rumbles by
I nod and smile at those monuments
as one greets old and revered friends

Reflected in the glass
preserved on celluloid
their changeless expressions
stay unmoving and soft.

Ricapito

A Day Best Not Remembered

On a happy day
when even alley cats smile
you took away my only dream
carried with me like a scapular
knowing all the time it was mine
like my nose or my voice
something no one else could claim
not even God
But that day
I handed you a daisy
alive, white, with a black eye
staring like Polyphemus
and you handed me back
shreds, white, torn.

Second Wave

HARVEY HAMMOND COMES HOME

Harvey Hammond comes home
Beer night with the boys after work,
His body rolling around,
Hitting against the table, chairs,
And the stove.
Harvey Hammond sloshed
Glad work is over
Building match-stick houses
Moving earth,
Chuggalugging the earth right down
The throat.
Harvey Hammond took the long, long piss,
Swaying a bit,
Closing his eyes a bit.
Harvey Hammond fell into bed
And found Alice
Insulated against the pillow,
A worn night-gown
Choked against a crooked leg.
The beer kicked Harvey Hammond's sex,
And he muzzled and whined like
A lonely dog.
Alice snored
And snored

(continued)

Ricapito

And snored.
Harvey Hammond tried again
Crawling on, digging his heels in the sheets
Until Alice's thighs opened with a groan.
Alice dreamed and woke to a
Balloon coming to rest on her,
The fat of his belly swaying,
His cock slipping out
"Sorry, dear."
When he came, Alice groaned again
And felt him roll over,
His ass lighting the night
Like the moon
And his breath fouling the room
Falling deeply into the four-walled
Confines of his sleep.

Second Wave

INDIANA WINTER

We send up funneling
puffs of smoke
our eyes made smaller
by the cold staring at us
its face covers a smirk.
This year winter comes hard,
creeping with the pace
of a tank
and lays a film of
ice on the lake.
All this cold and ice
and wind cutting us up
I sense a curse
wished on us, strange and strong.

Ricapito

JAPANESE TOURISTS IN FLORENCE

You don't have to wear anything on your head anymore.
Soon they'll let you in half naked to gape at Christ.
The Japanese, wearing Nikons like yokes, smile.
Their way is older than ours!
Their eyes peel paint from the murals.
A guard closes his eyes,
His vigilance a penance.
Why do they come, in straw hats,
from every direction imaginable?
At seven they roar into the *osterie*.
Do they know that ten years hence
It will all be a blur
Punctuated by discarded check books
and misplaced postcards?

Second Wave

MID SIXTIES

Can those raised in off-key
Baptist hymn singing
know the pungent smell of incense
at benediction?
Or those in prayer shawls,
know the black pit isolation
of the confessional?

You can't spend your lifetime at pool side
when you've listened to the drone
of brimstone hell
or entrusted the Virgin
with your profound childish wishes.

You can't shake hands with priests
dressed in Hawaiian shirts,
their toes squirming
through thonged sandals.

It is a disadvantage
to have spent winter mornings
shivering in the corner of a rectory
in cassock and surplice.

Ricapito

What Was Missing?

What was missing?
Watch the crown
spill forth its best hopes
tarnished urns
clanking hollowly
panes of glass cracking slightly
What did I miss?
Where did I miss it?
My walk is heavy.
I am Willy Loman
carrying my hopes in heavy cases.
This has been a sad decade
counting the time in near misses,
rejections, and disguised no's.

Second Wave

My Horn, Now Only Shiny

I have been in this club
hundreds of times
in different cities,
late into the night,
into the early hours of the day.
The walls have been pushed out
with heavy sounds,
notes bouncing off the tables.
In the thick curling smoke
The music swims in my head
like a mixture of winds
and I must wait for it to subside
leaving behind in its wake
remnants of love, hate, anger.
During the day the club
is a coffin.
The walls are blank.

Ricapito

NEVER TO FORGET

This is a day when
The heat grows in corners of my mind.
Now, I sit in a room
Your memory a shadow on the wall
Growing smaller
Ready to swallow me
With its definitive wink.

In the ground the pebbles try to shake themselves
Loose from the iron-bite cement.

Of your kisses I only remember
The taste of raspberry
Lit by your playful fire.

Second Wave

PITTURA

Blues move like a sullen, slow landslide, lava

Reds sleep dejected
their illumination unplugged through
some vandalism

Yellows try to cry out
but someone has cut their vocal cords.
We hear only their frozen,
paralyzed gestures.

Blacks close murderously in
until the painter staggers
and falls to the ground.

Ricapito

POEMS

There are poems
like carts
rattling along a street
studded with uneven stones

or gilded ones
their recesses filled with
puffy velvet chairs

And others
filled with reason and thought
oh so heavy
and like pre-Columbian ships
tip over into nothingness
with a single whisper.

Second Wave

POLISH MASS, CHRISTMAS MORNING
BROOKLYN, NEW YORK, 1996

They came from Lodz, Warsaw, Crakow,
sitting in worship in the lower church.
The crowds part as the
young man,
red beard, deferential manner,
enters
then disappears behind an oak paneled door
only to emerge
in a white surplice
a red cross embroidered on the front.
Kids in Nike sneakers
praise the Virgin in Polish,
their dress is a composite of Europe and America.
If the figures in the crèche could talk,
they would speak Polish.
Between prayers people talk, gossip,
and interrupt to respond to the boyish priest.
As they pray some weep.
Whom have they left behind?
Wierze w Boga, credo in unum deum.
Yes, they do believe
strongly, unflinchingly.
They were born in the wrong time.
Earlier they would have been among the Christian martyrs,
torn apart in the Coliseum, yet remaining steadfast.
Ojcze Nasz
Their heads are high.
They are saying "We are Polish before anything else."
When the priest cracks the Host
some crack in the soul.
But they have *Ojciec Swiety,* His Holiness,
                    (continued)

Ricapito

he is the father of us all.
And they belt out a song full of passion.
At the end they file out, fulfilled,
to walk, talk, smoke.
Kids run to the playground.
The bearded young priest
goes into the little red car
and drives off to another church.

Second Wave

REVELATION

Humming a song.
It came as a surprise
Since I never could recall you ever singing.

Tragedy had become your daily mode.
A series of deaths, people in black,
Veils covering their faces,
Processions of family and friends,
Grieving relatives.
Crying was universal
There were years of grieving,
No songs, no music.
If we laughed, we hid it.
Going to the movies was heretical.

When I heard the tune
Hummed from your lips
I felt sunlight.
We had finally finished serving our time.

Ricapito

THE NEVER-ENDING SEA

A thousand feet away
Four bodies bathe in miles of surf,
Four heads, just specks from where I sit.

Indifferent, pale Algerian homes,
Like fields of wild mushrooms,
Soak up the autumn sun.

The suction of a magnetic sea
Draws those specks, just bodies now,
To the pit of its waterfall inferno.

The gloating surf, its appetite content,
Slaps encrusted sand castles,
Castles of a child's play.

The sea
Undisturbed,
Blue and clear,
Covets human treasures,
Piled one atop the other
In its marine cemetery.

At night the scalloped hills have reason to fear
When Neptune rises out of the sea to swallow the earth.

Second Wave

SEX INDULGENCE

Sex
covered with a silk scarf
in the late afternoon
dinner done
like Arabs
lolling with love for dessert

Sex
a game for hidden time
displaces selves
only on the outside
glowing
fearful to step inside
In the first hours of the evening
we dress like embarrassed strangers
and go on our way
having played our game
we pick up the left-over
candy-wrappers of ourselves.

Ricapito

SIXTY YEARS LATER

Sixty years later
you recalled how bitter it was
your sister was chosen
not you.
Although you hoped against hope,
your father's word was iron.
You lowered your eyes in obedience.
"Your life is to marry and have children.
Paola will take holy orders."
You thought it was a death sentence
you didn't want to marry
you wanted to save yourself for God
and the children that passed
through you felt the anger
as they screamed for air.

Slowly, you stirred your coffee,
and as your son,
I felt the throat closing
with smothered tears.

Second Wave

SOUTHERN LADY

Her fingers hold the cup daintily,
porcelain against porcelain,
her hair and makeup fixed,
a smile on her face.

She crosses her legs,
her hands flatten her dress
against her legs.

As she talks
the smile flutters ever so correctly.
The day wears on,
her smile falls a bit.
She speaks of forebears
who came to the land.
They broke ground
and built their fortunes,
all of them white.
Yes, Uncle Harris,
a pillar of the community.

She is active in her church,
Wednesday night bridge,
the Junior League.
She smiles,
but her eyes do not.

Ricapito

The Synagogue of Florence, Italy
Dachau

Hold hands and don't let any sounds come in your ears.
Look up imploring the Divine.
The weight of wisdom is in your eyes,
Your beards are filled with stones,
Your curls ringed with history.

Walk slowly, silently to your graves,
Strung together hand in hand like beads.
Stop! Take hope and respite.
Your silence is a passion and an enigmatic law.

Second Wave

VIETNAM 2

Vietnam is a word.
Like lace, intricate, baroque curlicues,
Elephant grass cutting your cheek,
leeches clinging to your sweaty skin.

Who is he,
the old man cleaning pots, cadging cigarettes?
One day on Tet in Danang
he came to life
firing an automatic
like he was born with it.
The old man with baggy-assed
pants, squinting hard.

I want to go home.
I want to go home.
Before all the blood leaves my chest,
before the light leaves my eyes,
the blank space growing larger, white, then grey.

Ricapito

Never Worn Wedding Dress
White with Train, Size 8

Your word,
That's all it took for me to dream
Down the aisle
Slowly, my father already in his cups,
Mother sniffling into a hankie.
I would be stately and aristocratic, although by nature
I am not.
And at the end of the aisle
You'd be there
Looking better than Robert Redford,
Slow and stately.

The dress sits in its box wrapped in tissue paper,
The color is going like a leaf yellow at the edges.

Second Wave

CHRISTMAS AT REST HAVEN ACRES

No one less than ninety,
They drift in and out
Of various stages of life
Watching Oprah,
Most of them in another world,
Remembering their youth in bayou homes,
Spanish moss.
Oprah leaps and screams,
And the audience acts like someone just
Won the lottery.
Prim servants carry trays
Of cakes at tea time.
School with nuns and a weekly
Visit of a priest to explain sin.
A woman moans a sound.
The skin is parchment.
A woman looks up,
One eye clouded gray.
It is Christmas Eve, and she says,
"Is it you? Is it you?"
How's the dog? Does she remember me?
You came. So nice you came."
I glide away out of her clouded sight
To visit someone who whines tearfully,
                        (continued)

Ricapito

"I'm so alone. They don't call."
"They will, they will," I insist.
I walk circuitously to avoid
The lady who by now is nodding happily,
"You came,"
And Oprah sings Jingle Bells.

Second Wave

GOLDEN AGE

Everybody spoke Italian
Landlord, fruit peddler,
The pharmacist neatly dressed.
Good Italian, that is,
Everybody said it was high class.
The laundry man spoke in a gruff voice,
But in Neapolitan dialect.

Shopkeepers did not have names.
They were the Calabrese, the Barese, the Sicilian.
My father spoke Italian
To the insurance man who had been
A *ragioniere* in Naples.
At dusk you heard
Giuseppe, Giovanni, Attilio, Vittorio, called to supper.
Even the Jewish boys, Chaim, Isaac, Saul, David, understood.

Golden age was when Donato
Came the third week of October with grapes or
The third week of July with tomatoes.
Coming home from school
I saw grape crates lined against
The wall where Donato had left them.
He would come back to
Get his money. Not right away. No rush.

It was when people
Responded to the weight of grief,
The keening of pain by holding a hand,
Waving a fan to cool.
It was acceptance of God's will.
When my father died
They came from fifty nearby houses,
My uncles and cousins,
To kiss his cool forehead.

Ricapito

BEHIND THE COUNTER AT SCHERZ'S BAKERY

I was twelve the first time I saw his arm.
He was dressed in a baker's white suit, flour sprinkled all over him.
Instead of a yarmulke he wore a baker's white cap.

He rubs his fingers along the numbers tattooed on his arm.
The numbers sail lazily, his fingers walk:
    5 the turns he took to avoid the authorities,
    1 stern as a lance, a Prussian at attention,
    7 his slouch around the gnaw of hunger in his belly,
    3 the grimace of those he saw in pain,
    2 the sliding of a body to the ground
       when a bullet slammed into his head.
These numbers are the code of his life.

Second Wave

HEARING AND SEEING

The deaf don't have to hear the dropping
of dishes from a tray in a cafeteria,
or the buzz of inane talk
or the killing hiss of gossip.
You don't have to hear
the hypocrisy behind sanctimonious pleadings.
You don't have to hear somebody
say that of course he loved you
but that was then
or the Highway patrolman
who's real sorry to tell you this
but they were speeding and
there was liquor in the car
and it never had a chance
once it slipped and skidded
right into an unmovable oak.
He was real sorry because
they were all killed instantly.
Sorry Ma'am.

I will see things in silent slow motion.
I will sense the passage of time,
the reverberations of movements,
the beating of leaves in the storm and wind,
the quiet time inside my body
that does not move.
Life will dance before my eyes
and at night
the bodies will lie down
to rise up again
when the sun blinds our eyes.

Ricapito

BUDDHA IN CHURCH

A Buddhist in cinnamon robes
Sits in Santa Maria Novella,
His hands folded
Impassive,
The Virgin Mary has turned away
From the horror of her Son's
Death.

The cross
Sends awkward shadows across
The altar.
Outside the cornice
Saints pray and angels
Are in ecstatic flight.

On Christ's face
A fly has come to rest
Forever.
The Buddhist smoothes his robes
And gazes in deep meditation
Until
He is elsewhere,
Lost on a mountainside,
At the foot of a gigantic
Statue of Buddha.

Second Wave

INDIANA SUMMER NIGHT

to Phil Appleman

After the last car has turned off the road
Its lights paralyze all life in its way,
The night comes down harder.
Cicadas electrify the air in a long streaming hum.
Crickets chirp some indecipherable message.
The leaves? The trees?
They stand, the green now banked to black.
Rabbits and skunks on borrowed time inhabit
The only world they will ever know.
Everything at once alive and free,
Free to run
Free to sing
Free to screech
Until the dawn creeps up slowly,
Silences the world,
And sends squirrels scurrying into trees.

For us the day has begun.

Ricapito

ON JEWRY

Men in chains, their eyes are lowered.
A death sentence is stamped on their arms.
Together they moan chants of tradition and desperation.
Scattered by winds they rise like crows
held together by their fright,
then swoop down to stand fixed in the place of their afflictions.

Softly, like somnambulists they walk to their deaths.
Lord, thy name is forbearance!

Outside, miles of Jews queue up.
The executioner, like an usher, takes tickets with a smile.

Second Wave

Making Poetry

Crows call
telling
there is so little time left.

On the ground
I lie transfixed,
an arrow piercing
my throat.

My fingers scratch the last poems of my life
on blades of grass.

Crows persist with their calls,
and the sheen of their plumage
glistens like
mortal sin.

I have finished.
After the sun goes down
and the night has come and gone
the dew will have
destroyed my last words.

Ricapito

After Fray Luis de León

You can fall through the universe headlong
and never hit anything out of place.
Every sphere twinkles
against the darkness and
Mars glows.
How it holds together,
I can travel
undirected, a messenger making calls,
now here, now there.
There is no time,
nothingness against my cheek.
Everything near yet far.
Objects sail by
without captains to guide them,
floating, unimpeded,
certain in their flight.
This is the great machine of the world.

After it was done
you could hear God step back
to admire the work.

Second Wave

MENIAL MAN

Menial man.

Sit.
The sun reflects its power
off the round
eyeglasses.

Your broom
—or is it a mop?—
lies in sullen dejection
too beaten to push the dirt
out from the cracks
in the cement.

Your lip curls
in happiness
—or is it arrogance and hate?

A car skirts by,
its horn
calls you
with a lazy drawl.
Time to flick the dust-cloth
—or clean a speckled wind-shield—?

Menial man.

Come smile at me
your grin of lazy contentment
                    (continued)

Ricapito

and curse my greeting
with words only a few understand.

At night you will whisper
songs, curses and idle threats.

Tomorrow
you will sit and
wait for the dirt.

The sun will not relent
But will peer with steadiness.
Your skin gets darker.

Second Wave

Phantom Garden

Sturdy, straight, the chairs await,
The table is bare.
From next door I hear pulsations but not the music,
a car, anonymous, drives by the house and disappears.
The sun steadily falls and bathes the garden in calm.
The dog watches the squirrel
walk on a wire.

Can you beat the final fall of the sun?
I wait for a knock at the door or a treading
on the path.
A leaf resists losing green to red then yellow,
the closure of a brutal season.

Your absence.

The chairs sit and the table waits.

Ricapito

OLD PHOTOGRAPH

Ninety years since you posed, a four year old, holding a purse.
You were adventurous even then.
They say you wandered away from home through the town
Down to the port, past boats,
Their peeling paint dyed by the sun.
Fisherman looked up as they mended holes
Made by tenacious fish in the nets.
You walked back up the streets;
You knew exactly where you were going.

The picture has turned color, almost obscuring you.
I have watched you age, now almost ninety four.

Through your dim eyes you remember that walk
And the fright etched on your parents' face
When you returned to the house.

Second Wave

ON THE LOSS OF VIRGINITY

It wasn't supposed to happen
this way.
It was supposed to be beautiful
like violins and flowers.
Instead she was cornered
on the bed against the wall
he breathing heavy on her cheek
the fumes of cigarettes
and cheap wine
conmigling in his beard
his words so trite
one hand pawing away
at her dress and pants
until her back was hurting
as he pushed against her
his hand moving in the dark
holding something
still murmuring
and she felt him squirm.
He looked like a snail
all scrunched up
his thrust was fast
then faster until she could feel
his ass wince in soiled satisfaction
then he slipped out
onto the rest of the bed
and slept
his breathing
lengthened into a light snore
She didn't want to come away from the wall.

Ricapito

A VISIT TO THE SYNAGOGUE OF FLORENCE

A round dome rises
amidst the white, grey, pink and black
marble of the churches,
a dome green with centuries of wisdom and history.
The gardens are quietly kept.
Inside the truck with the *carabinieri*
a young soldier from the provinces,
sinks slowly into an afternoon nap,
while a singer on the radio he keeps underneath the driver's seat
calls out to her lover
"Why, why have you left me?"

Inside, the cloister is different.
I see none of the saints I am
used to.
The walls are decorated with
designs that do not belong to
my world.
In front of a tabernacle
candles and cloths
of a deathly color
cover the sacred altars.
A star of David
has been delicately
embroidered into the black velvet.
It seems to say that it is alone.
A few miles away
a saint sitting atop a church
smiles down on the green dome.
He sheds his grace on all people.

Second Wave

SELF-EFFACEMENT OF A YOGA TEACHER

You reach for the infinite,
your muscles flow down
like a silver streak.
Your face reflects peace remote
from turbulent wind.
When you move barefoot
you glide and when you sit
your bones seem to fall
into place like the parts of a machine.
In your smile
is the ingenuousness of a child, playful.

All this ended
when you tore off a part of her
with a gun you didn't know how to use,
her flesh dashing against the wall,
and you yourself
dangling from the yellow kerchief
closing off light and sound.
until one final breath
and you are placid again,
your body flowing downward
in the infinite.
On the funeral pyre
the flames consume the good with the bad.
Your smile twists and turns black.

Ricapito

FIVE AUTOBIOGRAPHICAL POEMS

I
INITIAL VISIONS

Initial visions.
Standing at a window
the frost wrinkles at corners
glacial spider webs.
Snow falls on cars, trees.
Dead street lights
bear the weight of
crystalline drops.
People shuffle along
kicking up slow motion
clouds of snow.
They are wrapped in heavy coats.
Faces peer through mufflers.
A few steps away
my bed awaits me
square, soft, puffed-up
like cotton candy.
I crawl back into its warmth
and lose myself
in the folds of multiple blankets.

Second Wave

II
NEXT DAY

Next day.
I am at my window
Propped up by my father,
feeling his close and strong embrace.
The sun illuminates mounds of snow.
The street is alive with children
bombarding life with snow balls.
Everything feels the joyful thunder of snow
exploding on contact.
Sleds screech on the black-top
streets where the sun has challenged the frost.
No work today.
Everything frozen to a halt.
Joyful day.
From the kitchen
the smell of *caffè latte*
ensures the fact of my father's presence.
Initial visions.

Ricapito

III
WALKING ALONG

A cat carefully walked the fence
placing each paw.
It was a ball of fluff, so soft,
I raised it by its tail
swinging it in the air in a perfect circle
until the beast clawed me into awareness.
Fluffs were now barbed with terror.

Walking along the street
my hand touched
slats in a fence.
I counted twenty on Mr. Feola's fence.
"Look out, Sonny Boy, don't touch the fence.
Don't touch."
Then I looked up
a bit frightened of that leathery face
and his huge tummy hemmed in by an immense belt.
Later I learned to smile and whisper
"Va fare in culo."

Second Wave

IV
AT NIGHT

At night I wondered why I saw the phosphorescent picture
of a German Shepherd dog on the wall
with intelligent eyes and a stern muzzle.
I dared not look
for fear that he'd leap down on my bed.
Afraid, so afraid he was really there.
I have mastered some of these illuminated fears.
Today I wish for German Shepherds
large, wooly and intelligent.
At night other beasts torment my sleep.
I have grown, but only in part.

Ricapito

V
Family Feasts

Family feasts.
More than one.
Bowls of pasta tinted with orange-red sauce.
Talk, God, so much talk.
And loud.
Today my wife complains
I don't speak softly enough
at concerts and plays,
and other quiet happenings.
Family gatherings.
Mother, father, aunt,
Uncles and aunts,
cousins, sisters.
Everyone at the table
threading miles of spaghetti.
Meat balls are heaped in a dish
like stones in a pyramid.
Everything discussed.
Nothing resolved.
Talk, lots of talk.
At the end kids eat pastry
the cream smearing from ear to ear.

Second Wave

CRÍA CUERVOS PARA QUE TE SAQUEN LOS OJOS
[Raise crows so that they will pluck your eyes out]

What did we do wrong?
When did you separate yourself
From the boy we raised into
An indifferent adult?
You came home one day
And said you changed your name.
The old one didn't go well with
The self that you had wrought.
The old name was violent
And you had become a Buddhist.
When we ran into your friends
You introduced me as a furrier,
As if the money that sent you to Stanford
Was stolen.

Dry goods were good enough for my father;
They were good enough for me.
The hours I spent waiting for a call or a letter
I could have built a house with my hands.
To my grandchildren you introduced me as Mr. Smith.

When I got home and rang the bell
My wife asked, "Yes, who's there?"
"Mr. Smith," I said.

Ricapito

Under the Catalpa Tree

I have been here before
and I have talked into the night
and exchanged with my friends
our deepest secrets.
I have smoked long twigs
in hidden glee
in summer far from
the menace of school.

I cannot stay here long
otherwise I shall recall
all my life in that white clapboard house.
A leaf falls on my eyes
and covers my face; its
softness renders me mute.
Before I leave the garden
I run my fingers over the bark,
the furrows now grown deep,
One more time,
One more time.
Behind me the tree
telegraphs sadness
hidden deep as roots.

Second Wave

WITNESS

I

At first when I heard the key in the door
I barked
My master Bill came home with a friend.
They bantered and had a drink.
I watched the friend.
He seemed a bit unusual and had
a bizarre laugh.
Bill kept giving him beer,
lots of it
and he often touched him
in the face, a caress, really,
that the friend smiled oddly.
After more beer
Bill took him by the arm
and he and the friend
went to his bedroom
and shut the door.
I went to my pillow and waited
in the dark.

II

Later I heard angry voices, curses,
Bill told him to quiet down, and
Bill came out, fright etched on his face.
Friend's face ablaze, his face very red.
More curses and threats.
Bill stepped back, away from
the friend, his back to the piano and
                            (continued)

Ricapito

Friend took out a gun
and sent fire to Bill's head.
He fell down and the floor was red.
Friend looked at me right into my eyes.
Then he ran out the door.
I barked at Master. He was covered with blood
which I tasted, loving Master.
These were my kisses to him.

III

For a long time
Master lay there,
Not playing, not talking.
Someone came to the door,
And from then on
There were many, many people,
And Master was taken away
And I never saw him again.

I saw it, I saw it, I was
Trying to say,
But nobody asked.
Later I was put in a carrier
And then in a car.
We drove a long way.
People in the car wept
And told stories about Master.
But no one asked me. I knew. I knew.

Second Wave

KENT STATE

A frantic girl howls
"Sanity, sanity,
just a moment of sanity."

Rolled up in a heap
his blood paints a sign on the street
by which we shall make a turn
to senseless events.

Shadows flick off grey buildings,
The street is a long tunnel.

Bullets are copper lilies, rockets seeking their target.
They hit, then slow motion burrow
through the skin,
in great concentric circles,
leaving behind it
the odious smell of powder.
At the end
somebody on the way for cigarettes
or the evening paper gets it in the head.

He lies there
wrapped in a very common winter coat.
Those unlucky enough to see him
are left weeping and horrified.

Ricapito

First Communion

I

It was preceded by weeks of retreat,
a priest preaching fire and brimstone
to frightened children.
Days approached with black stealth
until First Confession.
Each day lines of children filed
into the church
led by a nun,
her starched coif a bird ready for flight.
She settled up front. Purity, she said,
to boys and girls whose fingernails were black
with dirt and soot.
She would pretend she was a priest
for us to practice the recitation of sins.
Each child moved forward,
struck with fear
would she really know the sins
imbedded in their souls?
Prim girls filed by, disappeared into darkness
and emerged as pure as they went in.
Bless me father for I have sinned…
behind the clouded plastic partition
the profile of the nun,
carved with Irish pride,
spoke low, purred, "What else, son?"
"I had bad thoughts about my brother."
"I stole fruit from the Sicilian's cart."
"Are you sorry you hurt God?"
"Yes, sister."
I marched out and saw the smirks of my friends
yet to enter.

(continued)

Second Wave

My sister walked in, her hands clasped neatly
She spoke quietly of angers and prayed
for her sick grandfather.
"Are you sorry you hurt God?"

II

Two hours before First Communion
Mamma laid out the white outfits,
a short pant suit for me,
a white pretend wedding dress for her.
Careful not to eat anything,
We had to receive.
We bustled around the house
and heard father mumble as he struggled
Making his tie.
We had to be perfect for their First Communion day.
But she felt sick,
Wasn't used to going this long
Without eating
Looked up at Mamma and she thinks
—no food, no water—
Today is First Communion day
She has to walk down the aisle
Hands clasped, a rosary folded about her hands,
As Sister said, step-by-step,
To receive her First Communion.
I stood as Mamma ran a comb through my hair.
I felt the new cloth of my white suit,
The silky long socks.
I held the black Missal,
A part of the things you bought for First Communion.
She had to drink water.

(continued)

Ricapito

Pity, Sister Mary said, now she can't take Communion.
Light passed out of my sister's eyes at that word.
But she could march in the church,
A stunningly beautiful white-faced girl with
Brown curls, a miniature Madonna.

III

Two years later
In her make-believe wedding dress
Her hands clasped, holding the same Missal,
A rosary bound around her waxen hands
She prayed the prayers
In silence and forever.
When they closed the lid of her coffin the last thing you could see
Was the pure white satin dress.

Second Wave

A FALLEN GOD

For seven days
I counted slow, expiring breaths,
occasional moans, and listened
to his hand forever smoothing sheets.

One time he called my name
and hugged me hard, as if to buy life.
He ran his fingers through my hair
and wept so hard
I felt the cracking of his soul.
He knew the end was near,
And worse that that
life was not the game he thought.
A nasty joke some said it was.

There he lies, so long, so cool, a fallen God.
No one hears my mother's tears;
Just the dull noise of one bead falling consumed upon another.

Seven days to create the world,
Seven days to watch the center of your world die.

I read that for Greeks
Gods did not die
But turned to trees and silver rivers.
A fitting end would be a proud oak,
But not here and not now.

Ricapito

A WEDDING
After a Poem by Yehuda Amichai
As Explicated by Chana Kronfeld

I

In the Mexican statuette
the couple stands in black tuxedo
and white wedding dress,
their faces skulls.
It is the end,
and perhaps it should be
that way,
standing together, dying together.

II

The war is on.
They are young but don't know it.
He got his tuxedo at the
used clothing store,
the castaway of a musician
or the legacy of a waiter.
She used her sister's wedding dress.
There was no time to have one made.
They posed stiffly for a photographer,
the picture now yellows in its frame

III

The Mexican dolls smile through their clenched teeth,
and laugh their way
together
into eternity.

Second Wave

About the Poet

Joseph V. Ricapito is a professor of Spanish, Italian, and Comparative Literature at Louisiana State University and holds the Joseph S. Yenni Distinguished Chair for the Development of Italian Studies. He holds degrees from Brooklyn College, CUNY, University of Iowa, and a PhD in Romance Languages from the University of California at Los Angeles. He is the author of *Florentine Streets and Other Poems*, published by Bordighera and recently he published his first novel, *Fratelli, A Novel*, with AuthorHouse of Bloomington, Indiana.

Ricapito's specialty is the Renaissance and the cultural and literary relations between Italy and Spain. He has written on the picaresque genre in the comparative context. He also teaches "Petrarch in Europe" in the Comparative Literature Program. He has also researched and written on spiritual literature in Spain, especially the work of Alfonso de Valdés. Ricapito has developed a course at Louisiana State University called "Italians in America," which has attraced many students, Italian Americans as well as non Italian Americans.

He lives in Baton Rouge, LA, with his wife, Carolyn. They recently celebrated their golden anniversary. They have two children, Frank and Maria Avadna, and two grandchildren, Giuseppe and Francesca.

VIA FOLIOS
A refereed book series dedicated to Italian studies and the culture of Italian Americans in North America.

JOSEPH RICAPITO
Second Wave
Vol. 52, Poetry, $12.00

GARY MORMINO
Italians in Florida
Vol. 51, History, $15.00

GIANFRANCO ANGELUCCI
Federico F.
Vol. 50, Fiction, $16.00

ANTHONY VALERIO
The Little Sailor
Vol. 49, Memoir, $9.00

ROSS TALARICO
The Reptilian Interludes
Vol. 48, Poetry, $15.00

RACHEL GUIDO DEVRIES
Teeny Tiny Tino
Vol. 47, Children's Lit., $6.00

EMANUEL DIPASQUALE
Writing Anew
Vol. 46, Poetry, $15.00

MARIA FAMÀ
Looking for Cover
Vol. 45, Poetry, $15.00
CD, $6.00

ANTHONY VALERIO
Tony Cade Bambara's One Sicilian Night
Vol. 44, Memoir, $10.00

EMANUEL CARNEVALI
DENNIS BARONE, ED. & AFTERWORD
Furnished Rooms
Vol. 43, Poetry, $14.00

BRENT ADKINS, ET.AL
Shifting Borders
Vol. 42, Cultural Criticism, $18.00

GEORGE GUIDA
Low Italian
Vol. 41, Poetry, $11.00

GARDAPHÉ, GIORDANO, AND TAMBURRI
Introducing Italian Americana: Generalities on Literature and Film
Vol. 40, Criticism $10.00

DANIELA GIOSEFFI
Blood Autumn/Autunno di sangue
Vol. 39, Poetry, $15.00/$25.00

FRED MISURELLA
Lies to Live by
Vol. 38, Stories, $15.00

STEVEN BELLUSCIO
Constructing a Bibliography
Vol. 37, Italian Americana, $15.00

ANTHONY JULIAN TAMBURRI, ED.
Italian Cultural Studies 2002
Vol. 36, Essays, $18.00

BEA TUSIANI
con amore
Vol. 35, Memoir, $19.00

FLAVIA BRIZIO-SKOV, ED.
Reconstructing Societies in the Aftermath of War
Vol. 34, History/Cultural Studies, $30.00

A.J. TAMBURRI et al
Italian Cultural Studies 2001
Vol. 33, Essays, $18.00

ELIZABETH GIOVANNAMESSINA, ED.
In Our Own Voices
Vol. 32, Ital. Amer. Studies, $25.00

STANISLAO G. PUGLIESE
Desperate Inscriptions
Vol. 31, History, $12.00

HOSTERT & TAMBURRI, EDS.
Screening Ethnicity
Vol. 30, Ital. Amer. Culture, $25.00

G. PARATI & B. LAWTON, EDS.
Italian Cultural Studies
Vol. 29, Essays, $18.00

HELEN BAROLINI
More Italian Hours & Other Stories
Vol. 28, Fiction, $16.00

FRANCO NASI, ed.
Intorno alla Via Emilia
Vol. 27, Culture, $16.00

ARTHUR L. CLEMENTS
The Book of Madness and Love
Vol. 26, Poetry, $10.00

JOHN CASEY, ET AL.
Imagining Humanity
Vol. 25, Interdisciplinary Studies, $18.00

ROBERT LIMA
Sardinia • Sardegna
Vol. 24, Poetry, $10.00

DANIELA GIOSEFFI
Going On
Vol. 23, Poetry, $10.00

ROSS TALARICO
The Journey Home
Vol. 22, Poetry, $12.00

EMANUEL DIPASQUALE
The Silver Lake Love Poems
Vol. 21, Poetry, $7.00

JOSEPH TUSIANI
Ethnicity
Vol. 20, Selected Poetry, $12.00

JENNIFER LAGIER
Second Class Citizen
Vol. 19, Poetry, $8.00

FELIX STEFANILE
The Country of Absence
Vol. 18, Poetry, $9.00

PHILIP CANNISTRARO
Blackshirts
Vol. 17, History, $12.00

LUIGI RUSTICHELLI, ED.
Seminario sul racconto
Vol. 16, Narrativa, $10.00

LEWIS TURCO
Shaking the Family Tree
Vol. 15, Poetry, $9.00

LUIGI RUSTICHELLI, ED.
Seminario sulla drammaturgia
Vol. 14, Theater/Essays, $10.00

FRED L. GARDAPHÈ
Moustache Pete is Dead!
Vol. 13, Oral literature, $10.00

JONE GAILLARD CORSI
Il libretto d'autore, 1860–1930
Vol. 12, Criticism, $17.00

HELEN BAROLINI
Chiaroscuro: Essays of Identity
Vol. 11, Essays, $15.00

T. PICARAZZI & W. FEINSTEIN, EDS.
An African Harlequin in Milan
Vol. 10, Theater/Essays, $15.00

JOSEPH RICAPITO
Florentine Streets and Other Poems
Vol. 9, Poetry, $9.00

FRED MISURELLA
Short Time
Vol. 8, Novella, $7.00

NED CONDINI
Quartettsatz
Vol. 7, Poetry, $7.00

A. J. TAMBURRI, ED. M. J. BONA, INTROD.
Fuori: Essays by Italian/American Lesbians and Gays
Vol. 6, Essays, $10.00

ANTONIO GRAMSCI
P. VERDICCHIO, TRANS. & INTROD.
The Southern Question
Vol. 5, Social Criticism, $5.00

DANIELA GIOSEFFI
Word Wounds and Water Flowers
Vol. 4, Poetry, $8.00

WILEY FEINSTEIN
Humility's Deceit: Calvino Reading Ariosto Reading Calvino
Vol. 3, Criticism, $10.00

PAOLO A. GIORDANO, ED.
Joseph Tusiani: Poet, Translator, Humanist
Vol. 2, Criticism, $25.00

ROBERT VISCUSI
Oration Upon the Most Recent Death of Christopher Columbus
Vol. 1, Poetry, $3.00

Published by BORDIGHERA, INC., an independently owned not-for-profit scholarly organization that has no legal affiliation to the University of Central Florida or John D. Calandra Italian American Institute, Queens College/CUNY.

www.ingramcontent.com/pod-product-compliance
Lightning Source LLC
Chambersburg PA
CBHW051709040426
42446CB00008B/789